YOUR PASSPORT TO
RUSSIA

>> by Douglas Hustad >>

CONTENT CONSULTANT

Olga Mesropova, PhD
Associate Professor of Russian
Iowa State University

CAPSTONE PRESS
a capstone imprint

Capstone Captivate is published by Capstone Press, an imprint of Capstone.
1710 Roe Crest Drive
North Mankato, Minnesota 56003
www.capstonepub.com

Library of Congress Cataloging-in-Publication Data
Names: Hustad, Douglas, author.
Title: Your passport to Russia / by Douglas Hustad.
Description: North Mankato, Minnesota : Capstone Press, [2021] | Series:
    World passport | Includes index. | Audience: Grades 4-6.
Identifiers: LCCN 2020001074 (print) | LCCN 2020001075 (ebook) | ISBN
    9781496684097 (hardcover) | ISBN 9781496688019 (paperback) | ISBN
    9781496684608 (pdf)
Subjects: LCSH: Russia—Juvenile literature. | Russia
    (Federation)—Juvenile literature.
Classification: LCC DK17 .H87 2021 (print) | LCC DK17 (ebook) | DDC
    947—dc23
LC record available at https://lccn.loc.gov/2020001074
LC ebook record available at https://lccn.loc.gov/2020001075

Image Credits
iStockphoto: holgs, 15, oonal, 13, raisbeckfoto, 14, sbelov, 16, TanyaSv, 21; Red Line Editorial: 5; Shutterstock Images: Altana8, 6, Denis Kabelev, 28, Elena Odareeva, 25, Filip Bjorkman, cover (map), Irina Burakova, 22, Iurii Osadchi, 27, mutee meesa, cover (flag), Natalja Nikolaeva, 19, Sunwand24, 20, toiletroom, 9, Ttstudio, cover (bottom)
Design Elements: iStockphoto, Shutterstock Images

Editorial Credits
Editor: Jamie Hudalla; Designer: Colleen McLaren

Printed in the United States of America.
PA117

CONTENTS

Words in **bold** are in the glossary.

CHAPTER ONE

WELCOME TO RUSSIA!

It is winter in Moscow. Cold air hangs over Russia's capital city. Snow piles against the red walls of the Grand Kremlin Palace. This is the official home of the Russian president. People bustle through Red Square on their way from work. Tourists visiting from other countries gaze at the famous **architecture**. The onion-shaped domes on St. Basil's Cathedral shine in the sun. People chat in cafés and eat their favorite foods. Some eat blini, which are like pancakes.

A HUGE COUNTRY

Russia is the largest country in the world by land area. It has many different landscapes. Frozen tundra blankets the north. Warmer beach cities line the coast of the Black Sea in the southwest. Russia's population has grown in size over many years. It includes different groups of people.

MAP OF RUSSIA

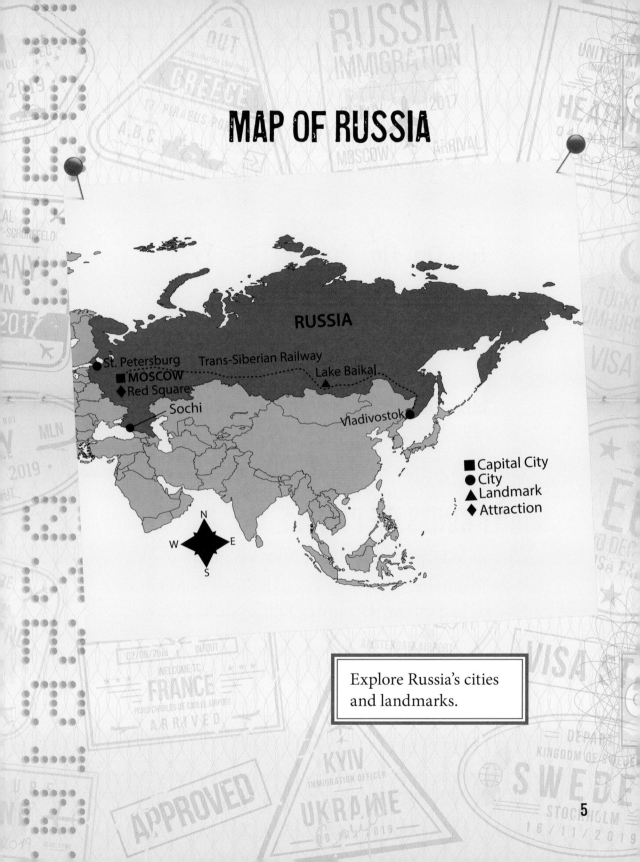

RUSSIA

St. Petersburg
MOSCOW
Red Square
Sochi

Trans-Siberian Railway

Lake Baikal

Vladivostok

■ Capital City
● City
▲ Landmark
♦ Attraction

N
W E
S

Explore Russia's cities and landmarks.

Аа	Бб	Вв	Гг	Дд	Ее	Ёё
a	be	ve	ge	de	ye	yo
[a]	[b]	[v,w]	[g,k]	[d]	[jɛ,jɜ]	[jɔ]
Жж	Зз	Ии	Йй	Кк	Лл	Мм
zhe	ze	i	ij	ka	el	em
[dʒ]	[z]	[i]	[ij]	[k]	[l]	[m]
Нн	Оо	Пп	Рр	Сс	Тт	Уу
en	o	pe	er	es	te	u:
[n]	[ɔ]	[p]	[r]	[s]	[t]	[əu]
Фф	Хх	Цц	Чч	Шш	Щщ	Ъъ
ef	kha	tse	che	sha	shcha	hard sign
[f]	[x]	[c]	[tʃ]	[ʃ]	[ʃtʃ]	
Ыы	Ьь	Ээ	Юю	Яя		
ii	soft sign	e	yu	ya		
[i:]		[ɛ]	[ju]	[ja]		

The Russian alphabet has 33 letters.

MANY KINDS OF PEOPLE

Russia is large in size. Just under 142 million people live there. That is less than half the population of the United States. The official language is Russian. Many people also speak Ukrainian, English, German, and other languages. Russia uses an alphabet called the Cyrillic alphabet. Some of the letters look very different from letters in the English alphabet.

The country is home to more than 190 different **ethnic groups**. One of these groups is the Tatars. They are from the Volga region. This historical area is in the east. About 5 million Tatars live in Russia.

FACT FILE

OFFICIAL NAME: ....RUSSIAN FEDERATION
POPULATION: 141,722,205
LAND AREA: .... 6.3 MILLION SQ. MI. (16.4 MILLION SQ KM)
CAPITAL: ....MOSCOW
MONEY: ....RUBLE
GOVERNMENT:...............................SEMI-PRESIDENTIAL FEDERATION
LANGUAGE: ....RUSSIAN
GEOGRAPHY: Russia spans the continents of Europe and Asia. It is bound by the Arctic Ocean to the north, Eastern European nations such as Ukraine and Belarus to the west, the Pacific Ocean to the east, and Asian countries such as Kazakhstan and Mongolia to the south.
NATURAL RESOURCES: Russia has oil, natural gas, coal, and timber.

CHAPTER TWO

HISTORY OF RUSSIA

Russia began as the small state of Rus in the 800s **CE**. It was in what is now western Russia. Rus is where the name *Russia* comes from. It means land of the Rus people. Rus grew into a powerful country in the **medieval** era. It did so through war. Mongol invaders from East Asia came and took over Rus in 1240. Rus split into several areas. Then a new country formed. It was near modern-day Moscow. This new country took back lands the Mongols had captured. It grew into the Russian **Empire**.

RUSSIAN EMPIRE

Emperors and empresses ruled for several hundred years. Russia's importance grew under these rulers. Many Russian writers, musicians, and artists became world-famous. But the empire started to weaken during World War I (1914–1918). Russia suffered many losses during this war.

Genghis Khan was a powerful Mongol ruler whose grandson conquered a large part of what is now Russia.

RUSSIAN REVOLUTION

Political rivals of the Russian **tsar** took control of Russia in 1917. A new **Communist** government took over. Russia became part of the Union of Soviet Socialist Republics (USSR) in 1922. Vladimir Lenin became its first Communist party leader.

TIMELINE OF RUSSIAN HISTORY

882 CE: Rus is formed.

1240: The Mongols take control over Rus.

1703: The city of St. Petersburg is founded.

1724: Tsar Peter the Great opens St. Petersburg State University.

1914–1918: World War I is fought. The Allies (Great Britain, France, Russia, Italy, and the United States) win.

1917: A revolution occurs that overthrows the tsars. Vladimir Lenin would later become the leader of the USSR.

1927: Joseph Stalin takes power.

1939–1945: World War II is fought. The Allies (Great Britain, France, the USSR, China, and the United States) win.

1947–1991: The United States and USSR fight for domination in what is called the Cold War.

1961: The USSR launches the first person into space.

1991: The USSR collapses.

2012: Vladimir Putin is re-elected president. He was first elected in 2000.

Lenin died in 1924. Three years later, Joseph Stalin took power. Stalin was a **dictator**. He killed many of his rivals. His laws made many people starve. But his five-year plans led the USSR to become modern and **industrialized**. Stalin's power expanded during World War II (1939–1945). The USSR and the other Allies won the war. The Allies included the United States.

But after the war, the USSR and United States became rivals. They were the two most powerful countries in the world. This rivalry was called the Cold War.

The USSR was made up of 15 republics. These included Russia, Ukraine, and Armenia. The republics fought for **independence**. The Union fell apart in 1991. The republics became their own countries. Today, Russia has a president. Presidents can stay in office for six years.

RUSSIA'S SPACE PROGRAM

Part of the Cold War was the space race. The United States and USSR wanted to beat each other in space exploration. The USSR had several early victories. It launched the first satellite in 1957. It also put the first human in space in 1961. But in 1969, Americans won the race to land a person on the moon.

CHAPTER THREE

EXPLORE RUSSIA

Red Square in Moscow has some of Russia's most famous sites. One of these sites is St. Basil's Cathedral. It has famous onion-shaped domes. St. Basil's was built in the 1500s. Tsar Ivan IV built it to celebrate a military victory. The cathedral overlooks the square.

Tourists can also see the red walls of the Grand Kremlin Palace. The Kremlin is the center of Russian government. Many people refer to the government by calling it "the Kremlin." Near the Kremlin is Lenin's Tomb. The Russian leader's body was preserved there in 1924. It remains on display for the public to see.

THE HERMITAGE

North of Moscow on the Baltic Sea lies the city of St. Petersburg. One of its most popular attractions is the Hermitage Museum.

The Kremlin was first used as a fortress.

The Winter Palace has more than 1,000 rooms.

The Russian empress Catherine the Great started the Hermitage's collection in 1764. The first pieces came from her own art collection. Today, the Hermitage has 3 million pieces of art. Only the Louvre in France is larger in size.

The Hermitage is a huge art museum. It has paintings, sculptures, historical **artifacts**, and other art. Some paintings come from famous artists. It has pieces by Leonardo da Vinci and Vincent van Gogh.

Tourists can travel across Russia on the Trans-Siberian Railway.

Many works are housed in the museum's Winter Palace. The Russian royal family used to live in the palace. Today more than 2.5 million people from around the world visit the Hermitage each year.

THE TRANS-SIBERIAN RAILWAY

A good way to see Russia's huge landscape is by train. The Trans-Siberian Railway is the longest railway in the world. It stretches 5,772 miles (9,289 kilometers). It runs from Moscow in the west to Vladivostok in the east.

At about 25 million years old, Lake Baikal is one of the oldest lakes in the world.

The railway first linked these cities in 1916. It took tens of thousands of workers. They built it over a span of 25 years! The entire trip takes eight days. The train crosses eight time zones.

LAKE BAIKAL

Tourists love to visit Lake Baikal. It holds more water than all five U.S. Great Lakes combined. It is the largest freshwater lake in the world! Freshwater lakes have little salt. Lake Baikal is also the deepest lake in the world. It is 5,387 feet (1,642 meters) deep.

FACT
The city of Vladivostok is in southeastern Russia. It is closer to Anchorage, Alaska, than it is to Moscow.

Lake Baikal is in southern Siberia. It is a popular stop on the Trans-Siberian Railway. The lake is famous for its clear water. People enjoy swimming and fishing in the summer. It freezes during Siberia's very cold winters. That makes it a great spot for ice skating.

CHAPTER FOUR

DAILY LIFE

Russia has huge cities and tiny villages throughout the country. People in Moscow often live in apartments. They get to work by subway or car. The subways and roads can be very busy.

Work looks different in Russia's rural countryside areas. Many people have jobs such as farming. Farmers have found success in growing and selling wheat. But many young people leave their villages in rural areas. They go to cities, where there are more opportunities. Many villages are shrinking because of this.

RUSSIAN RELIGION AND FAMILY

Russia has no official religion. But most of its people are Christian. About 72 percent of Russians are Russian Orthodox Christians. Nonreligious people make up 18 percent. Other religions include Islam, Judaism, and other forms of Christianity.

Many people in Moscow spend more than one hour in traffic on their way to and from work.

St. Basil's Cathedral is a Russian Orthodox cathedral in Moscow.

St. Petersburg State University is one of the top universities in Russia.

Family is very important. Multiple generations of a family often live together. Even when young people move out, they still come home often. In many families, grandmothers often look after their grandchildren. Grandmothers are called babushkas.

EDUCATION

Education is important to Russians. More than half of adults have a college degree. That is one of the highest percentages in the world. Free public school through high school is offered to all citizens. Children must attend school through grade 11.

Blini can be eaten with many toppings, including sour cream or fish eggs.

COMMON MEALS

Some Russian foods have become loved around the world. Beef stroganoff was developed in Russia in the 1800s. Then it became popular in the United States in the 1950s.

RUSSIA'S OLDEST UNIVERSITY

Russian emperor Peter the Great founded St. Petersburg State University in 1724. It is the oldest university in Russia. It is one of the oldest in the world. The university survived the Russian Revolution and two world wars. President Vladimir Putin studied there. Nine Nobel Prize winners have graduated from the university.

Beef stroganoff is a beef-and-noodle dish. It was named for a family of Russian nobles. Blini are a kind of pancake. They can be a dessert or a snack. People may put honey or sour cream on top of blini.

ZAPEKANKA

Zapekanka is similar to cheesecake. It can be made with savory ingredients for dinner or sweet ones for breakfast. This recipe includes ingredients for breakfast. With the help of an adult, you can make this recipe at home!

Zapekanka Ingredients:

- 1 pound of ricotta cheese
- 4 eggs
- 7 tablespoons of sugar, or 5 tablespoons of honey
- 2 tablespoons of sour cream
- 2 heaping tablespoons of corn starch
- 1 tablespoon of softened butter
- ½ teaspoon of vanilla
- Dried fruit (optional)

Zapekanka Instructions:

1. Preheat oven to 350°F (180°C).
2. In a large bowl, stir together ricotta cheese, egg yolks, sugar, sour cream, corn starch, and vanilla.
3. In a separate bowl, whisk the egg whites.
4. With a spoon, stir the egg whites into the cheese mixture.
5. Add dried fruit, if desired.
6. Coat the bottom and sides of a pan with butter to keep batter from sticking.
7. Pour the mixture into the pan. Place in oven and bake for about 30 minutes.

CHAPTER FIVE

HOLIDAYS AND CELEBRATIONS

Despite its name, New Year's Day in Russia lasts a whole week! People start celebrating on December 31. They gather with friends and family and welcome the New Year. January 1–5 is a holiday for most workers. Schools are closed too.

Victory Day is on May 9. It celebrates the USSR's victory over Germany in World War II. Most major cities in Russia have a military parade. The biggest one marches through Red Square. The celebration ends with colorful fireworks at night.

RELIGIOUS HOLIDAYS

The Russian Orthodox church follows an old form of calendar. So Christmas is celebrated on January 7. People have big feasts with family. They give gifts and go to church.

Many Russians gather for church services on Christmas.

People could not celebrate Christmas during the USSR era. Religion was banned at that time. Celebrating it is now a big deal.

CHAPTER SIX

SPORTS AND RECREATION

Many Russians take sports very seriously. The success of Russian athletes has made the country proud. When Russia was part of the USSR, the USSR was the best in the world in ice hockey, figure skating, gymnastics, and other sports.

FACT

The Kontinental Hockey League is one of the strongest hockey leagues in the world. Many of its players have represented Russia in the Olympics.

Russia has drawn worldwide attention for its ability in sports. Moscow hosted the 1980 Summer Olympics. Sochi hosted the 2014 Winter Olympics. Russia also hosted the 2018 FIFA World Cup.

Tatiana Volosozhar and Maxim Trankov won gold in pairs figure skating during the 2014 Olympics in Sochi.

Some students in
Russia join chess clubs.

CHESS MASTERS

Russians also enjoy chess. It first came to Russia in
the 900s CE. The country has had some of the greatest
players in history. One, Garry Kasparov, became the
youngest world chess champion at 22 years old!

Russia has many features for visitors to enjoy. There are lakes, railways, delicious foods, and stunning museums. It has bustling cities and vast wilderness. In all these places, people can learn about Russian culture and the country's global influence.

CHAPAYEV

Chapayev is a game similar to checkers. It is named after a famous Russian military hero, Vasily Chapayev. To play, you will need a checkerboard, 16 game pieces of two different colors, and two people.

1. Pieces of one color are placed on the last row of one side and the other color in the last row on the opposite side.
2. Players take turns flicking one of his or her game pieces at the opponent's, trying to knock one or more off the board. If the player's own piece stays on the board, he or she gets an extra move.
3. If the move doesn't knock a piece off the board, it becomes the opponent's turn. The game continues like this until there is only one color left on the board.
4. A new round of play then starts with the winner's pieces moved one row farther forward. By the time the game reaches seven rounds, the pieces will be next to each other.
5. From the seventh round forward, the loser must move backward. Once one opponent runs out of space for his or her pieces, he or she loses, and the game is over.

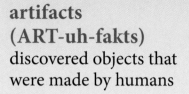

GLOSSARY

**artifacts
(ART-uh-fakts)**
discovered objects that
were made by humans

CE
CE means Common Era, or
after year one

**Communist
(KAHM-yuh-nist)**
having to do with a type
of government that owns,
controls, and distributes all
goods and property

**dictator
(DIK-tay-tuhr)**
a leader who has complete
control over a country

empire (EM-pire)
a large area ruled by
an emperor

**ethnic groups
(ETH-nik GROOPS)**
people who share a
common culture, race,
language, or nationality

**independence
(in-di-PEN-duhnss)**
the freedom a country has
to govern itself

**industrialized
(in-DUHS-tree-uh-
lyzed)**
introduced the large-scale
mass production of goods
to an area

**medieval
(mi-DEE-vuhl)**
a time period referring to
the Middle Ages, roughly
spanning the 5th to
15th centuries

tsar (ZAHR)
the Russian term for king
or emperor

READ MORE

Blevins, Wiley. *Russia*. New York: Scholastic, 2018.

Hopkinson, Deborah. *Where Is the Kremlin?* New York: Penguin Workshop, 2019.

Lanser, Amanda. *World War I by the Numbers*. North Mankato, MN: Capstone Press, 2016.

INTERNET SITES

BBC News: Russia Country Profile
https://www.bbc.com/news/world-europe-17839672

DK Find Out!: St. Basil's Cathedral
https://www.dkfindout.com/us/earth/landmarks-world/st-basils-cathedral

National Geographic Kids: Russia Facts
https://www.natgeokids.com/au/discover/geography/countries/russia-facts

INDEX

OTHER BOOKS IN THIS SERIES

YOUR PASSPORT TO CHINA
YOUR PASSPORT TO ECUADOR
YOUR PASSPORT TO EL SALVADOR
YOUR PASSPORT TO ETHIOPIA
YOUR PASSPORT TO FRANCE
YOUR PASSPORT TO IRAN
YOUR PASSPORT TO KENYA
YOUR PASSPORT TO PERU
YOUR PASSPORT TO SPAIN